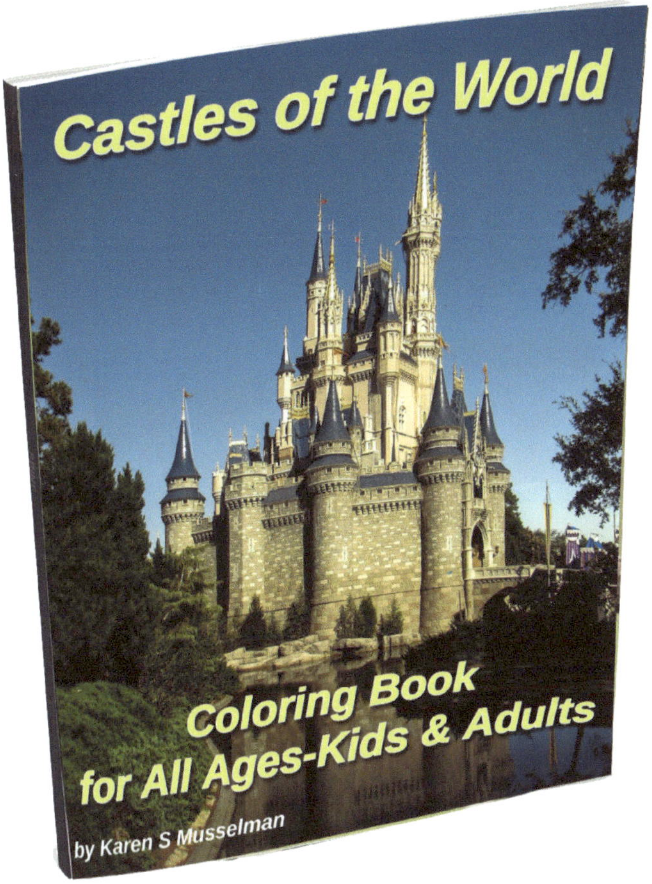

Castles of the World Coloring Book
for All Ages-Kids & Adults

40 coloring pages of some of most beautiful
and luxurious castles in the world.

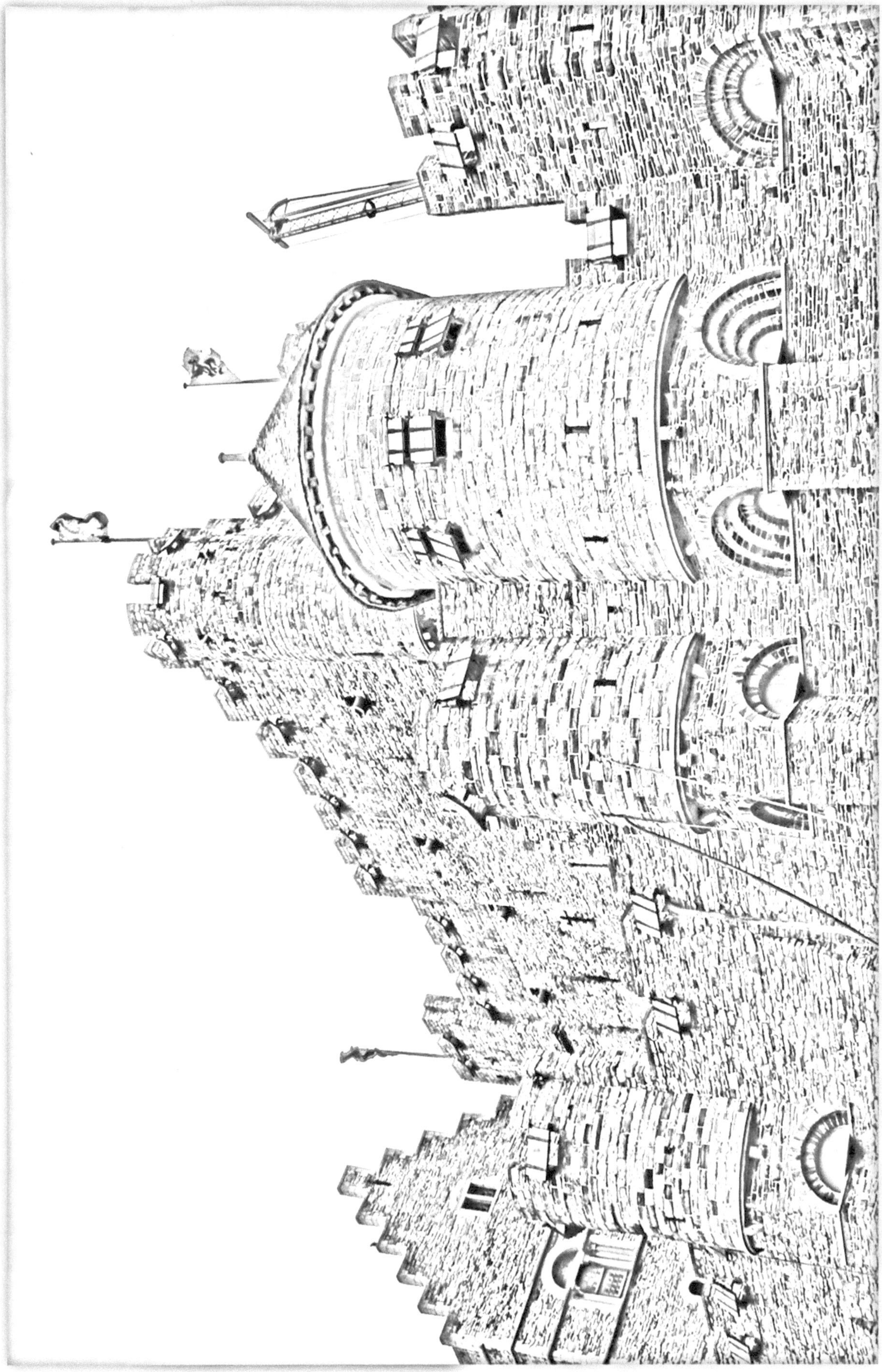

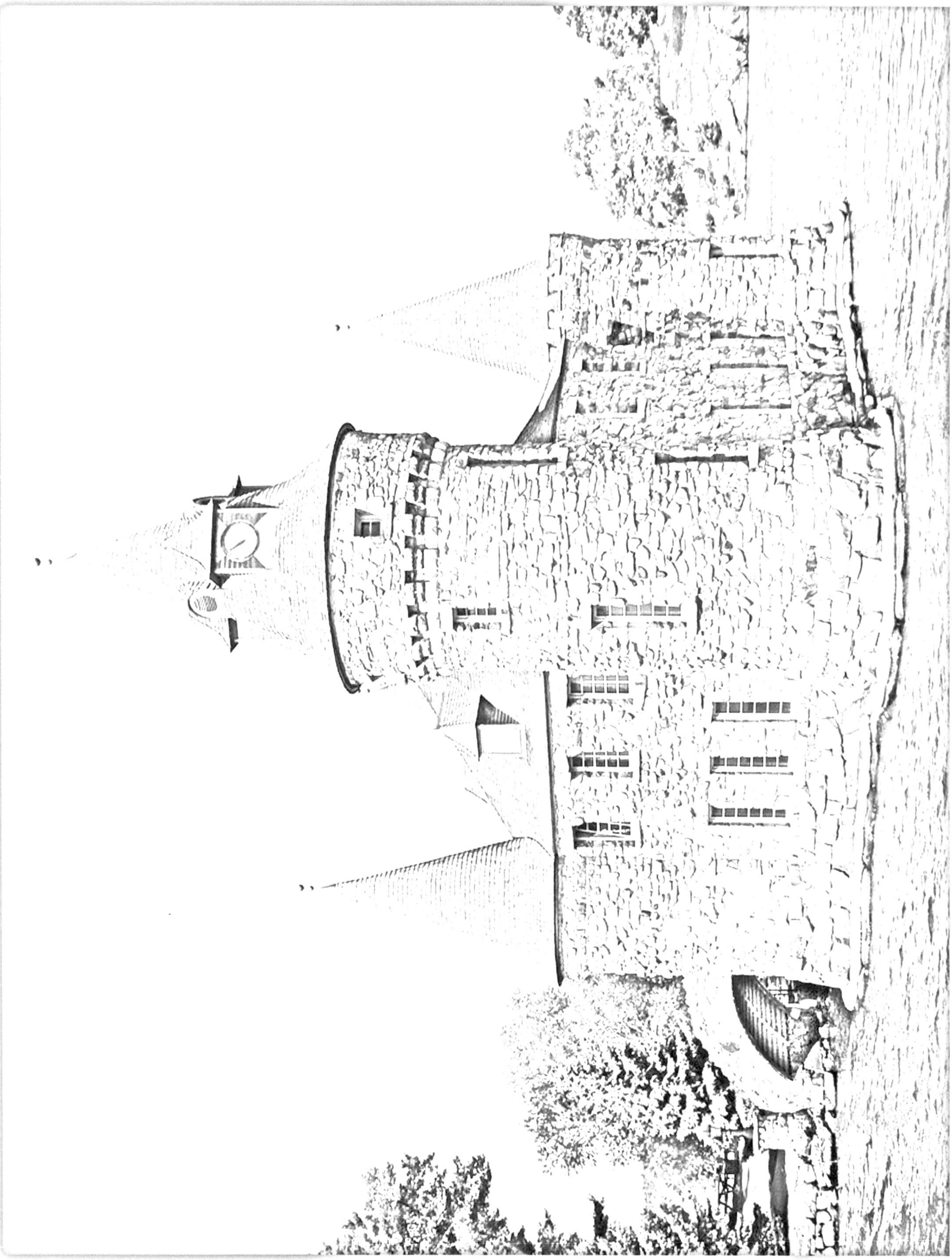

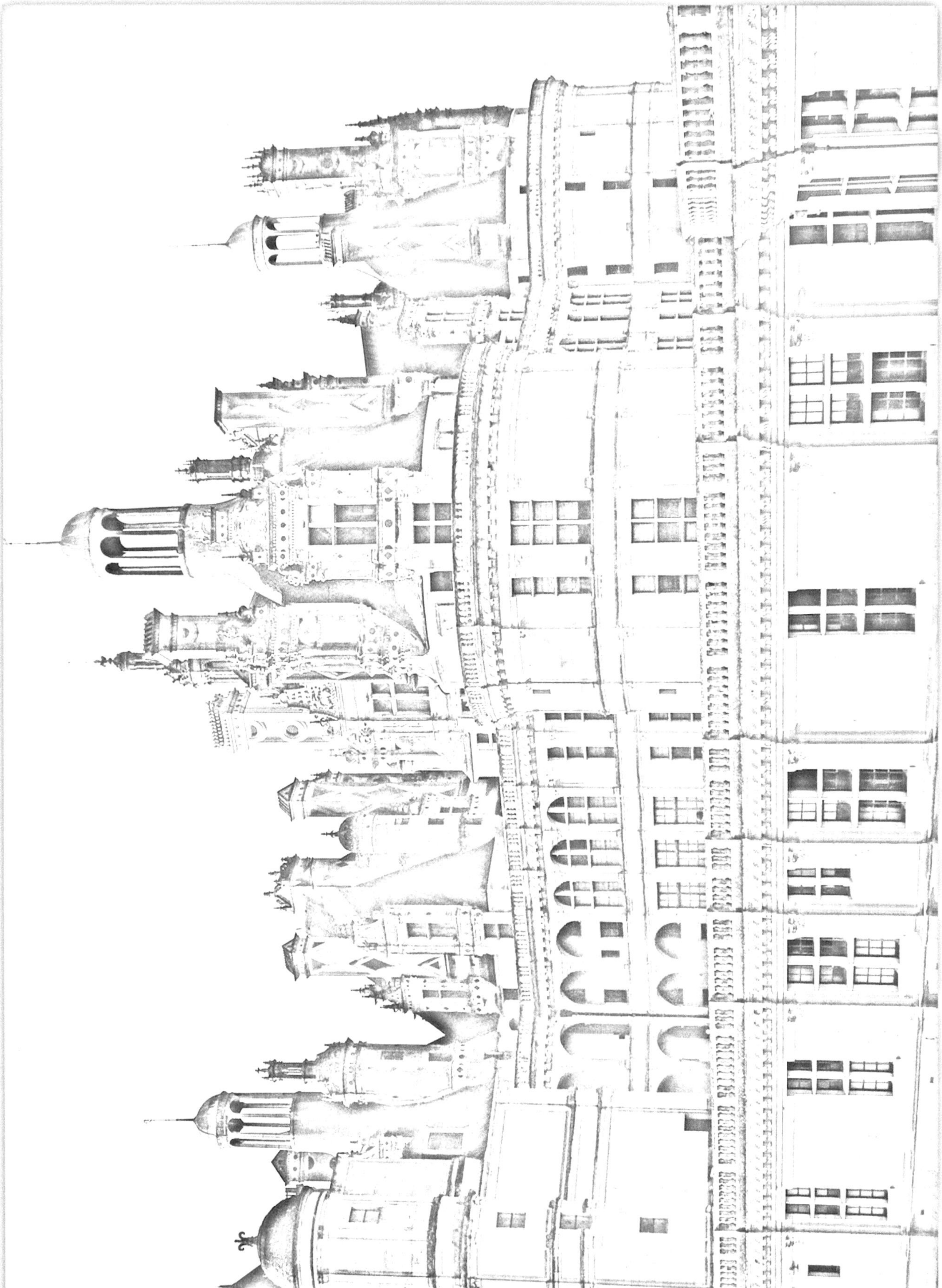

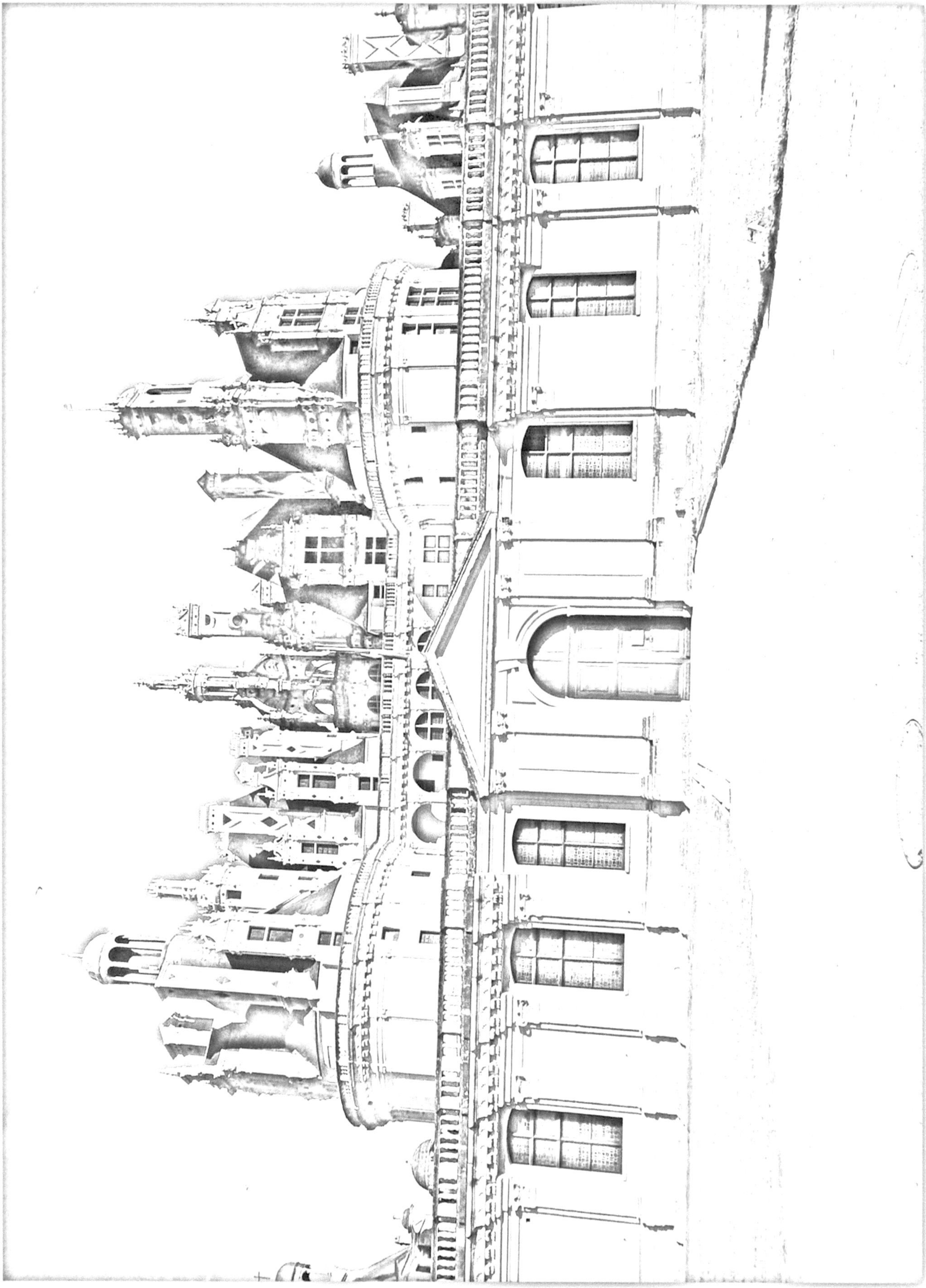

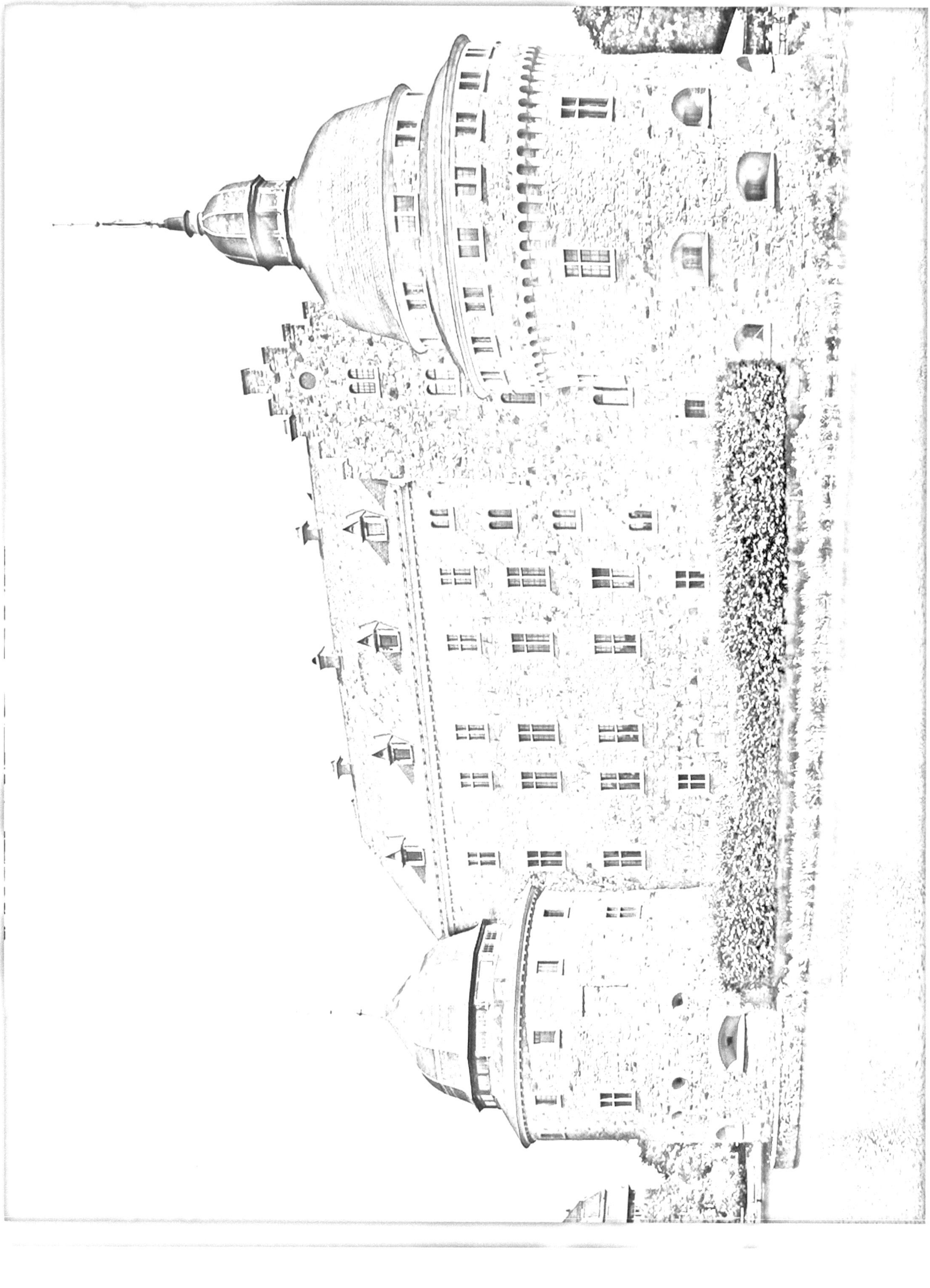

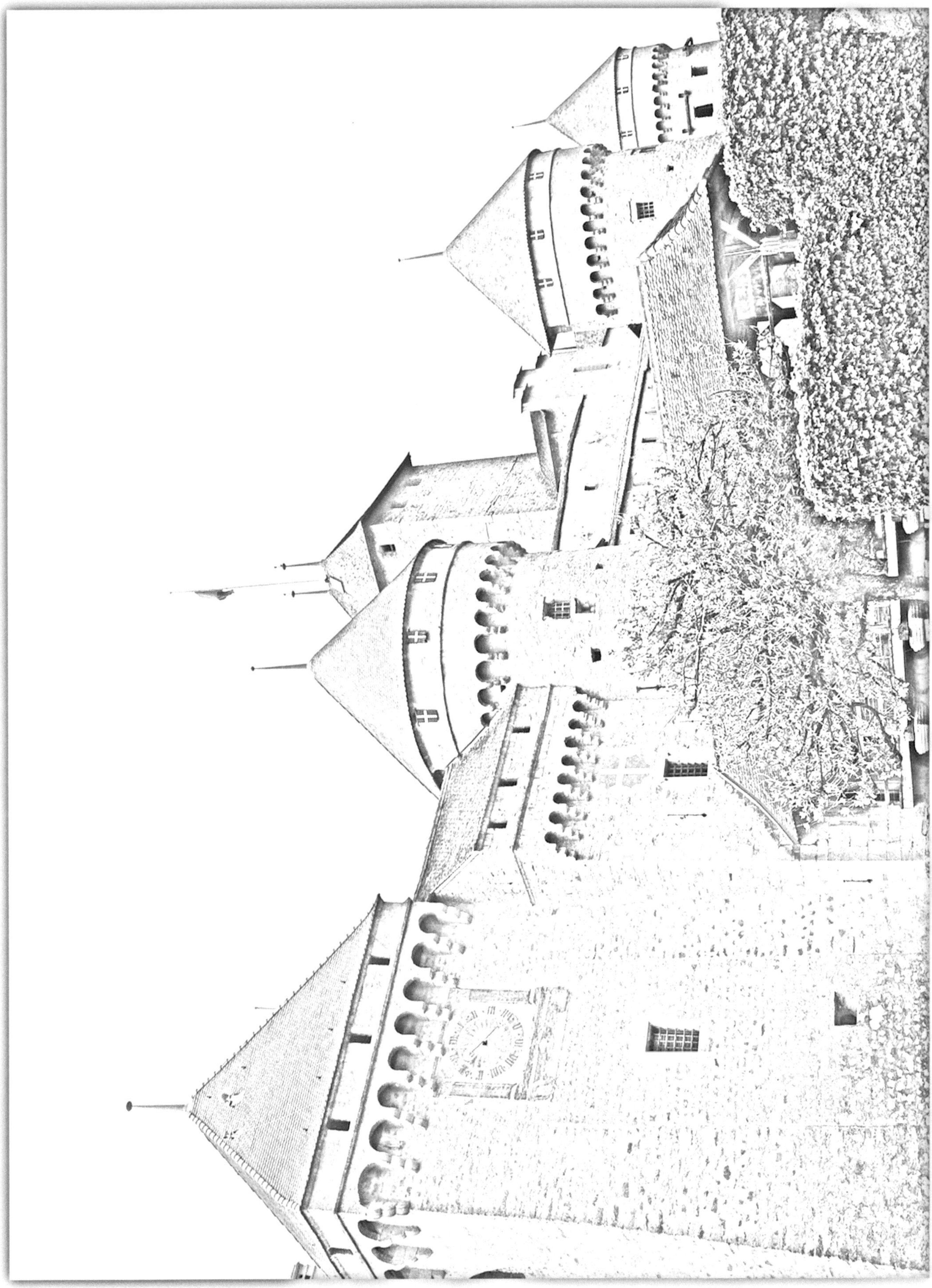

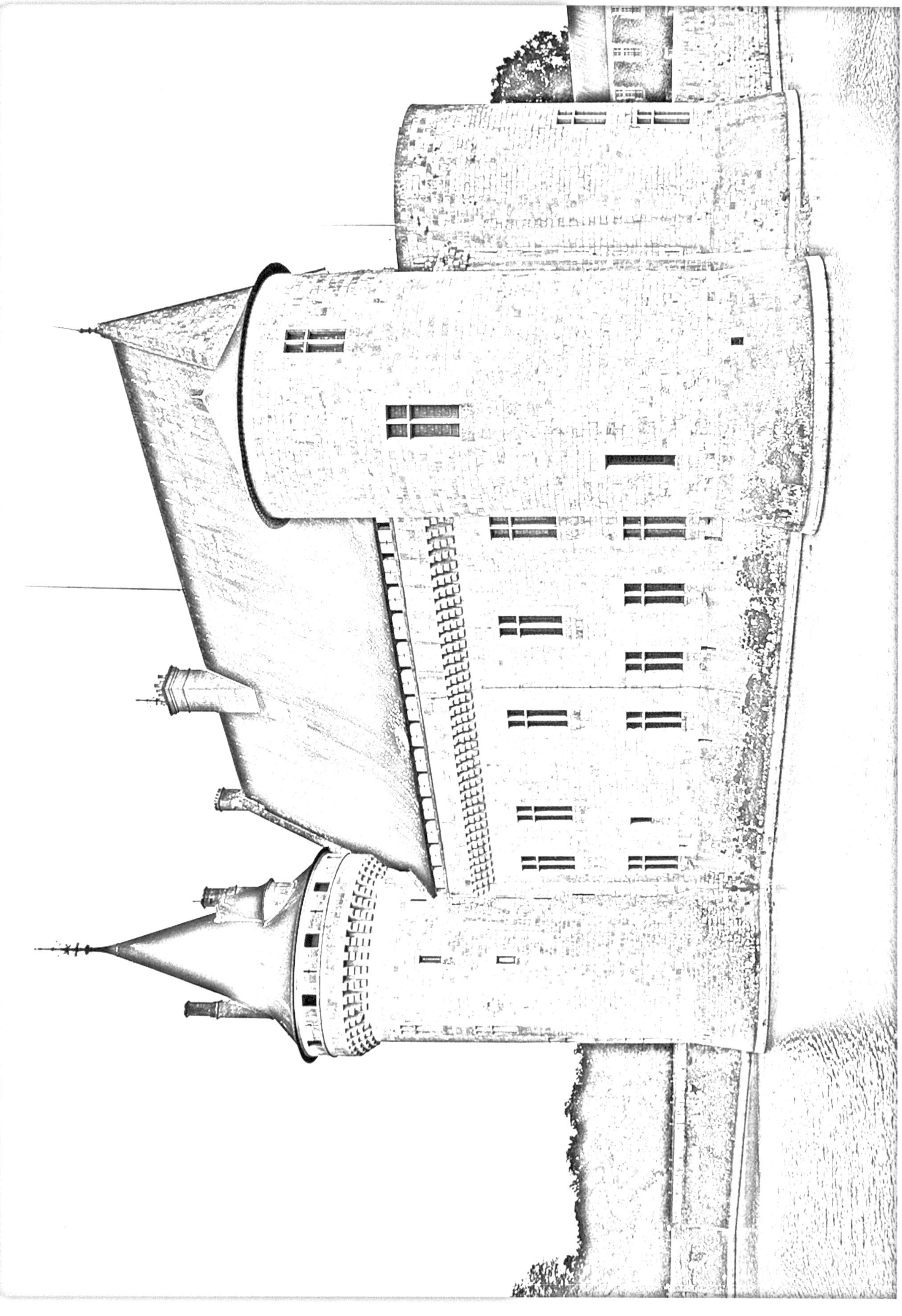

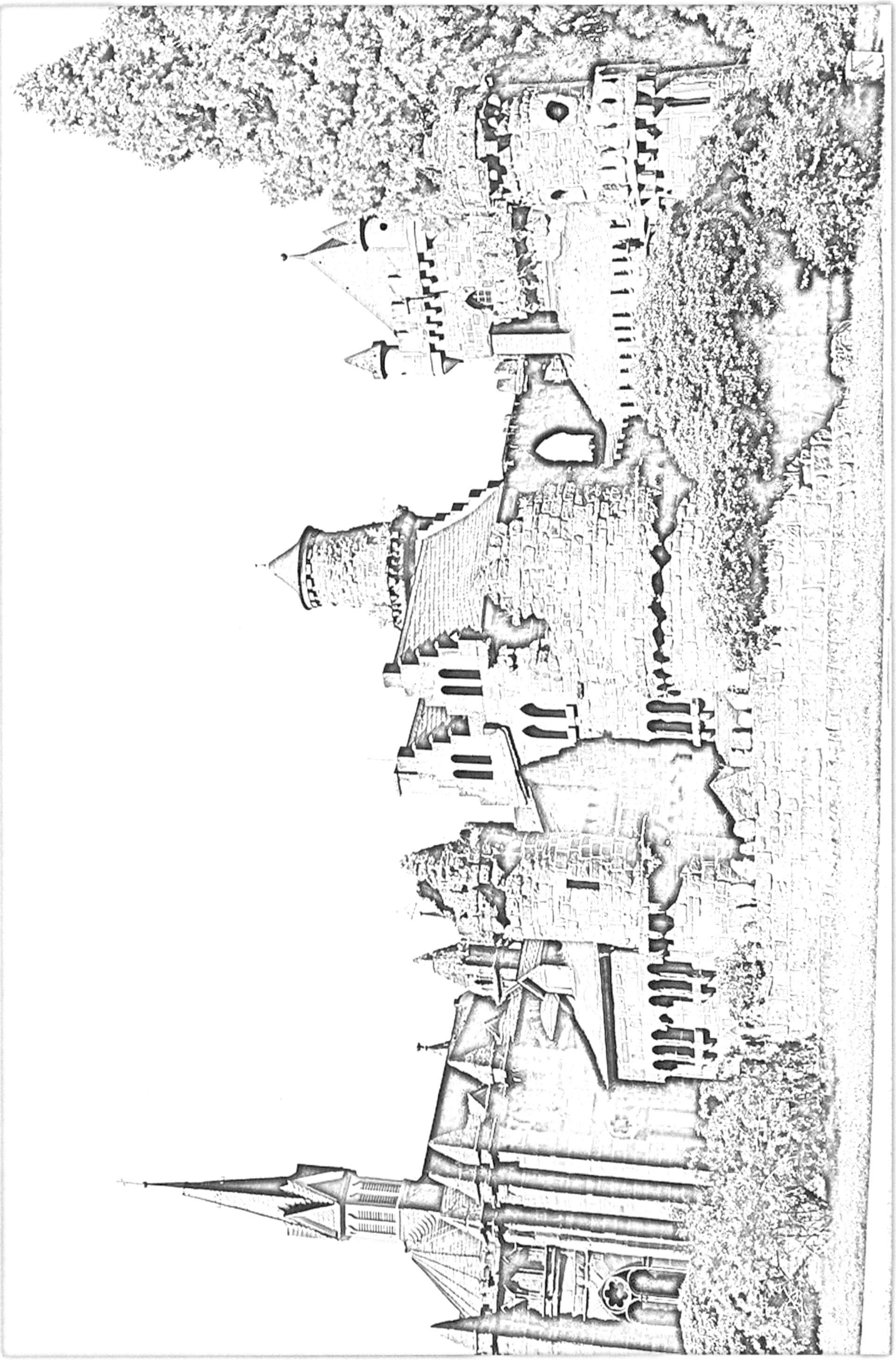

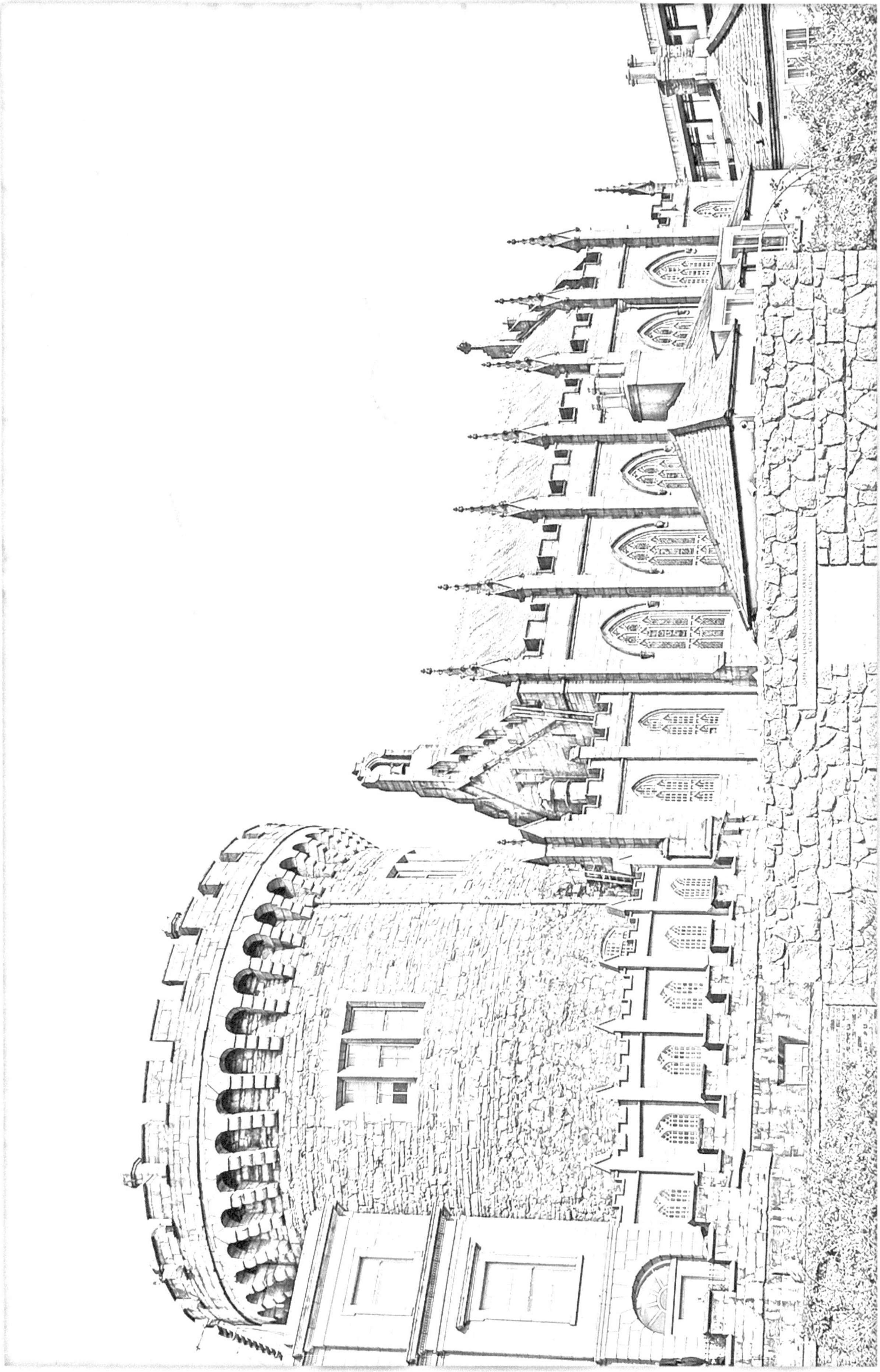

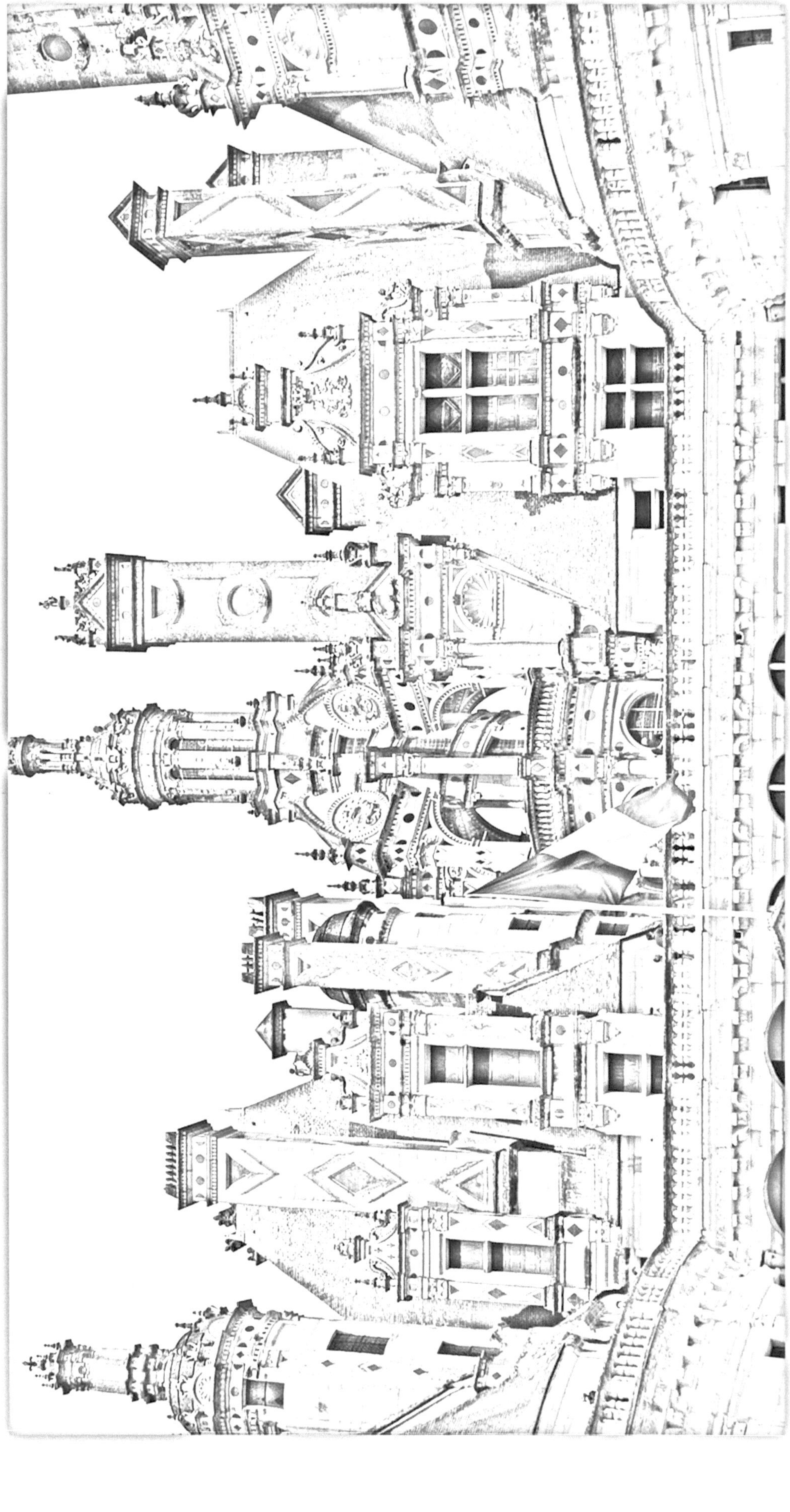

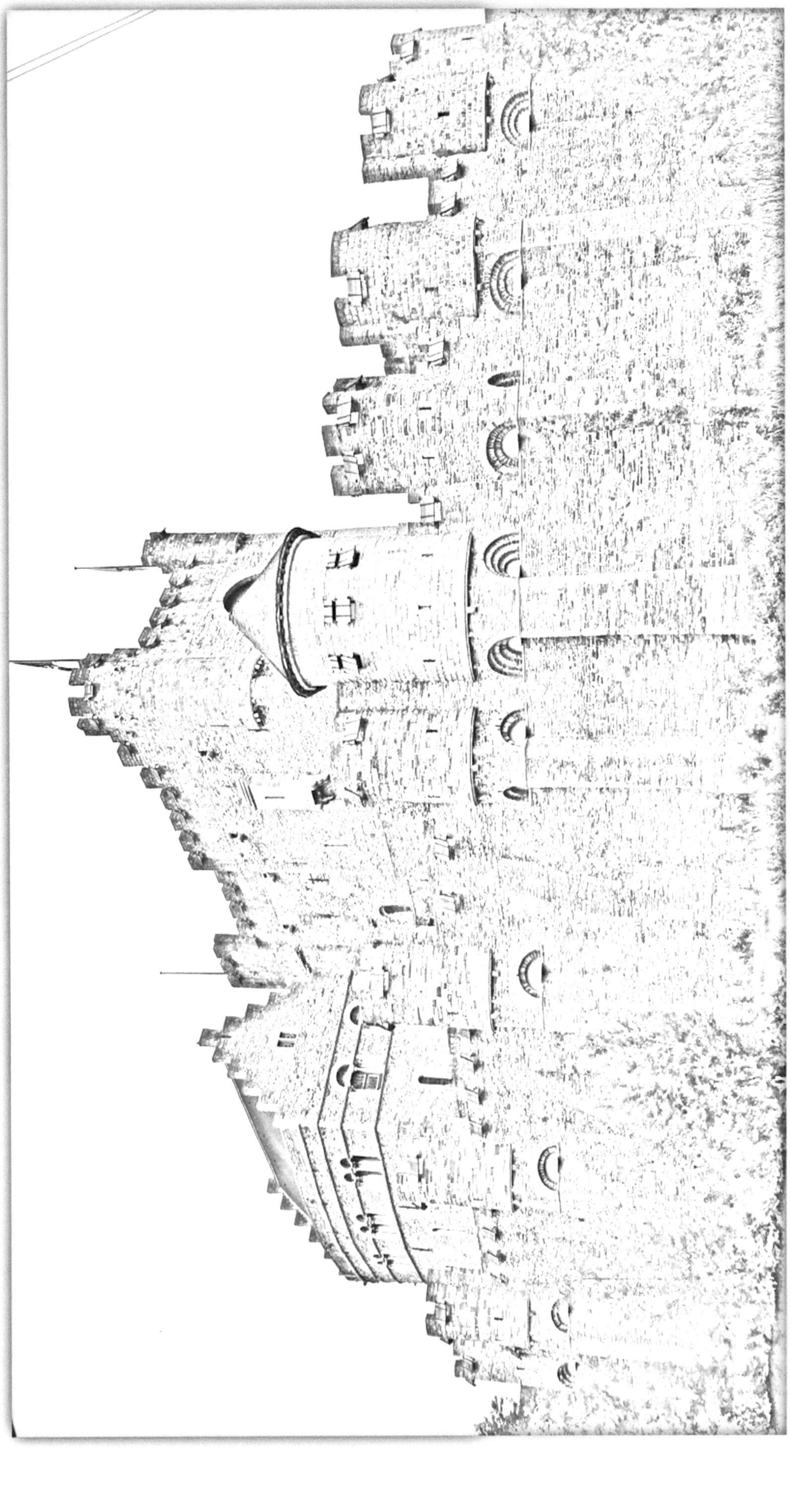

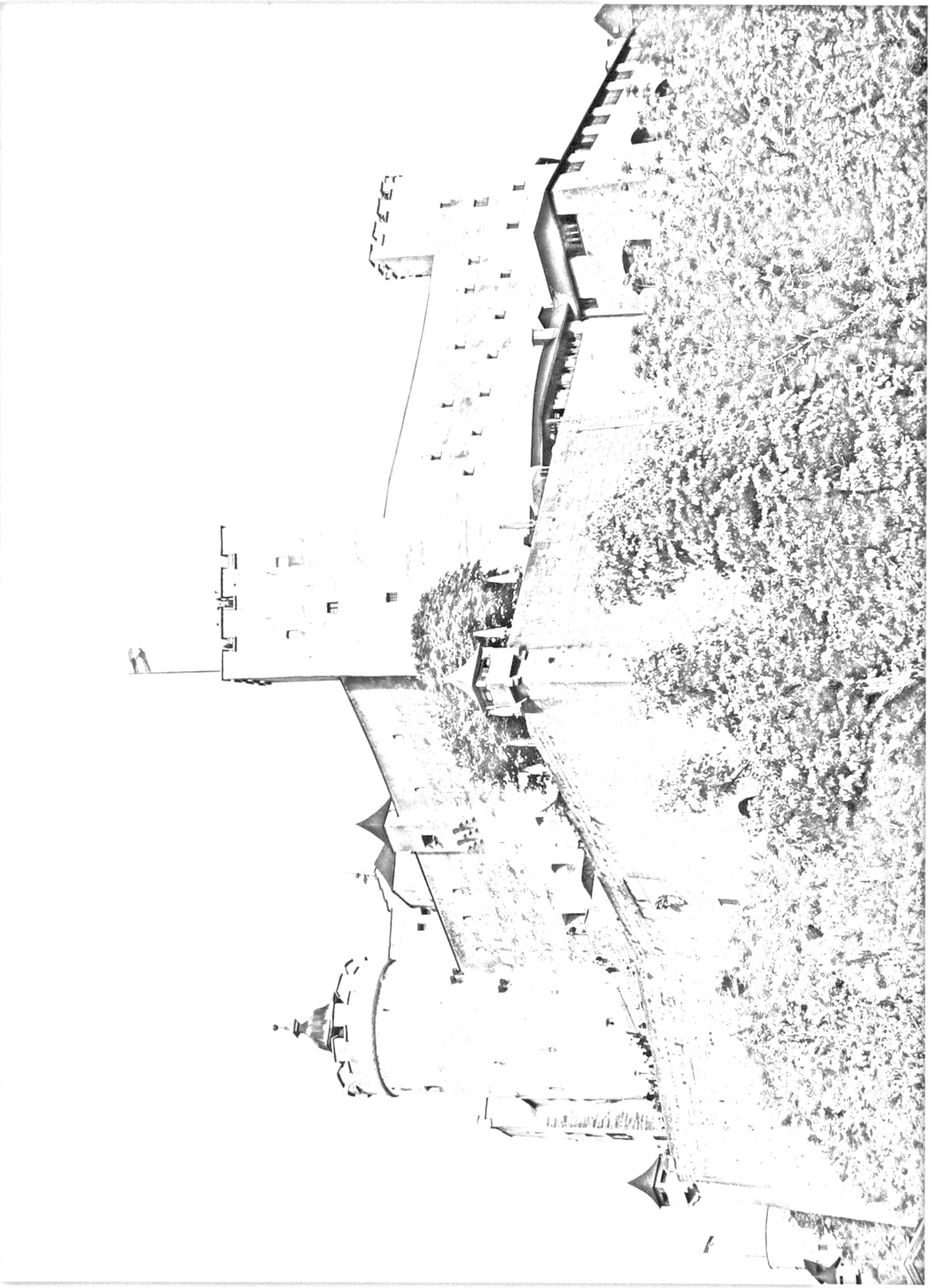

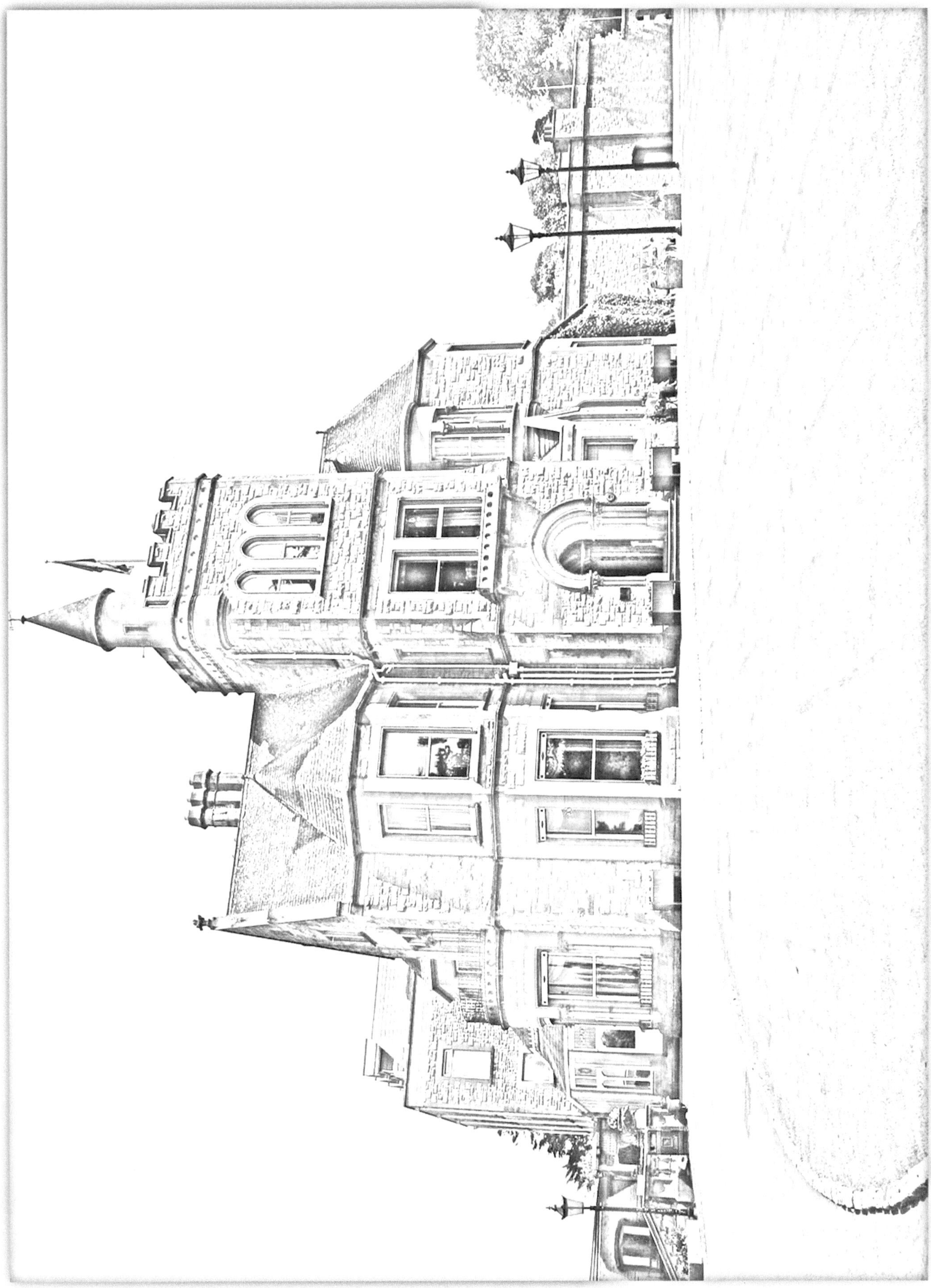

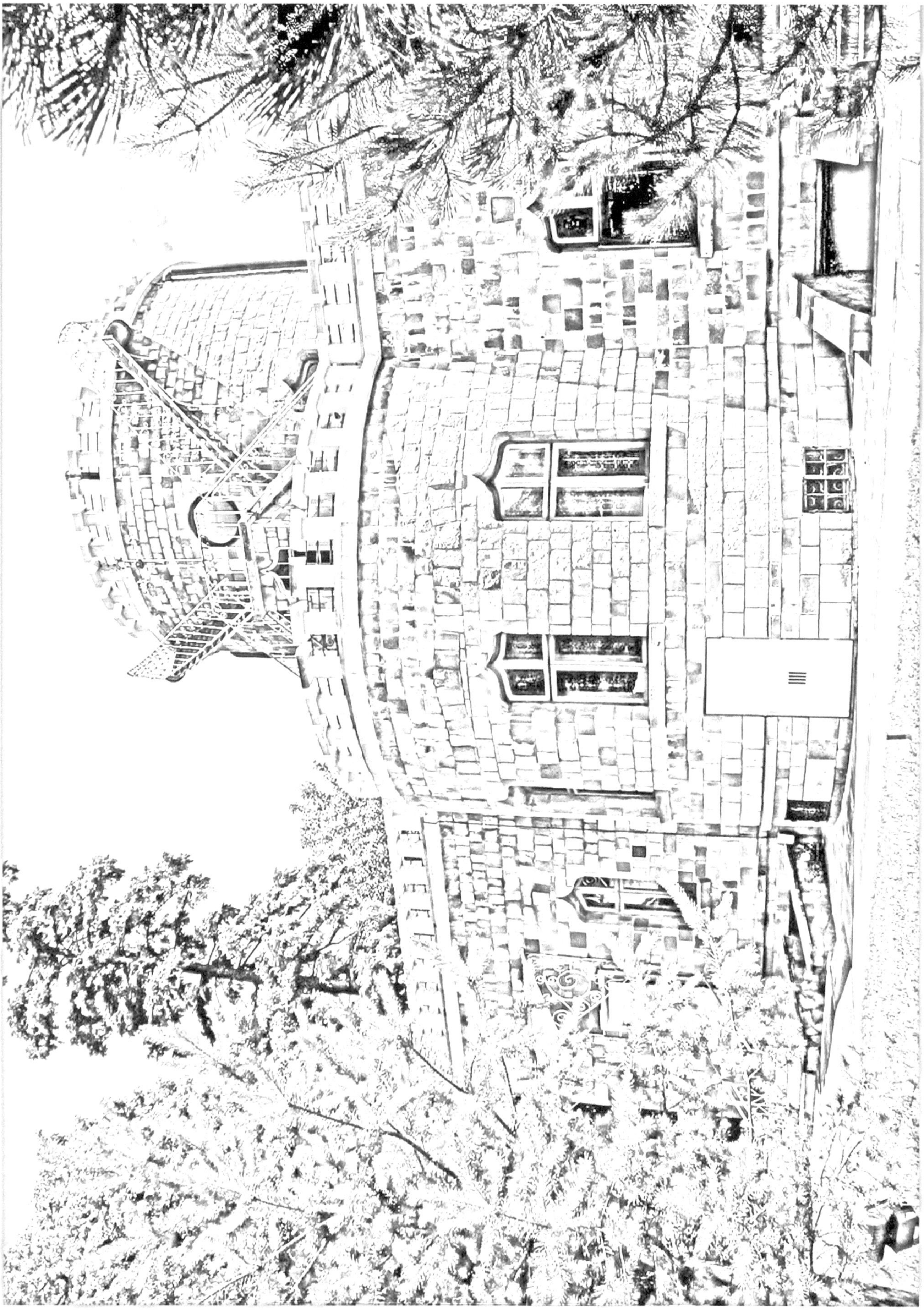

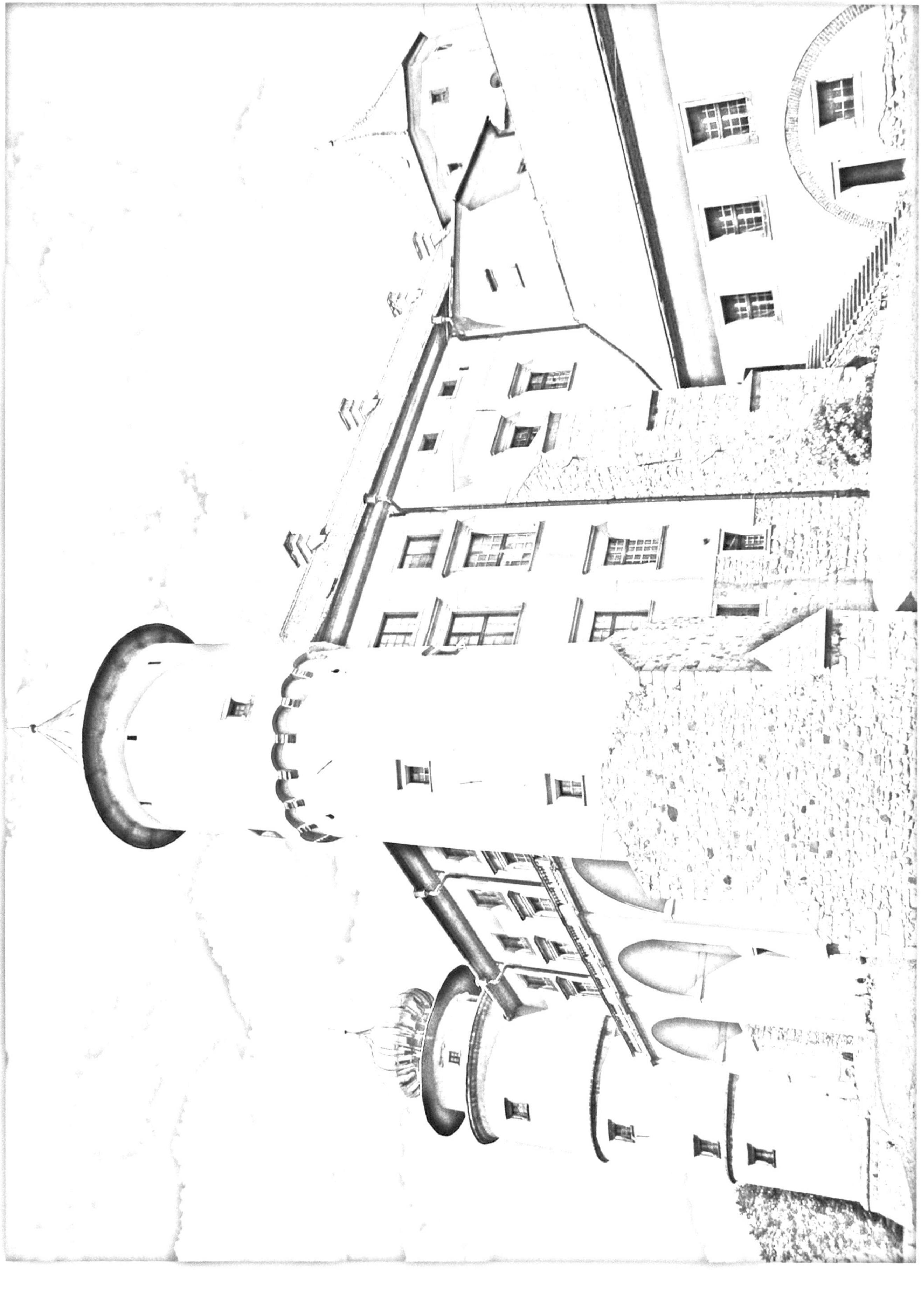

Friedensburg

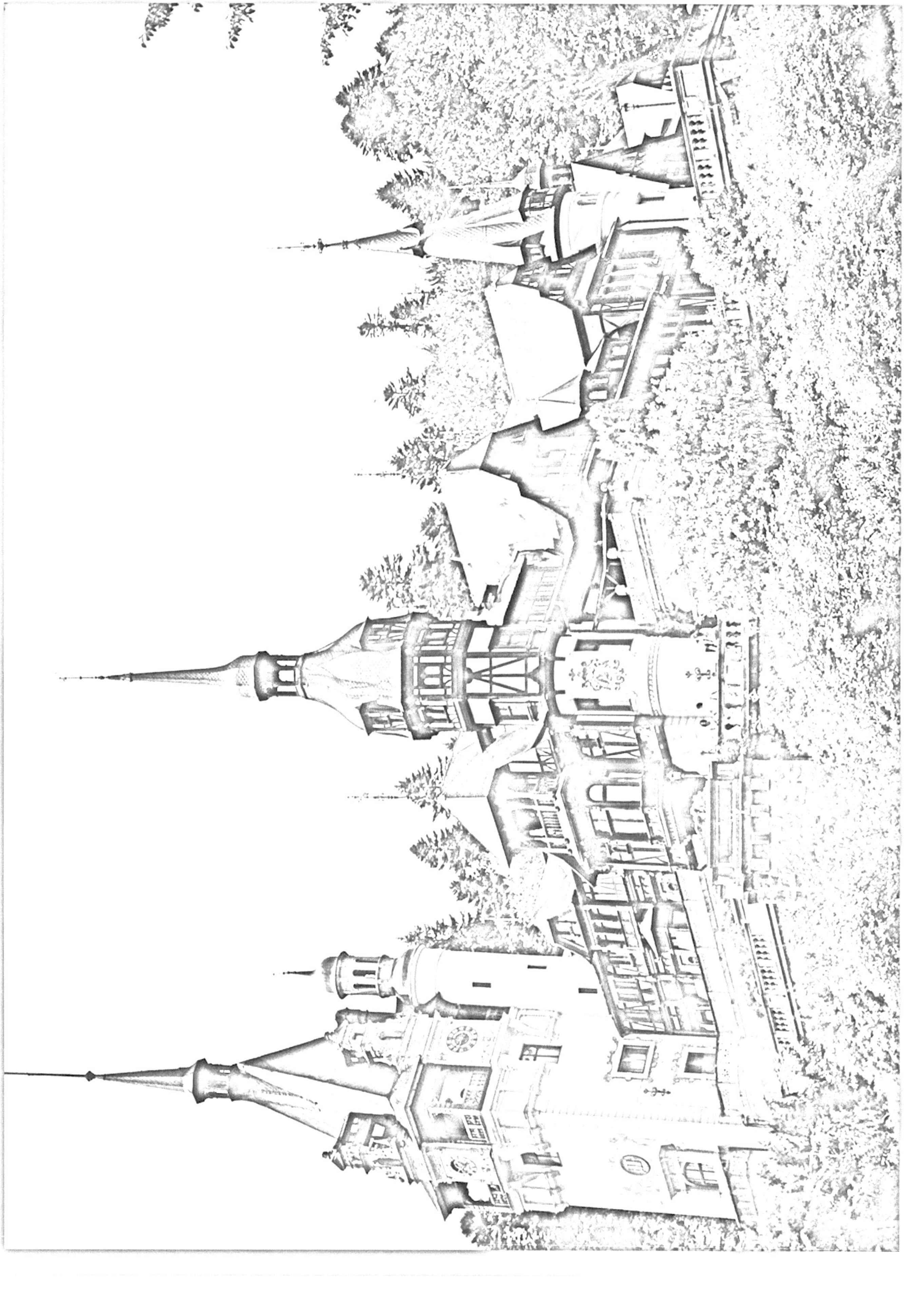

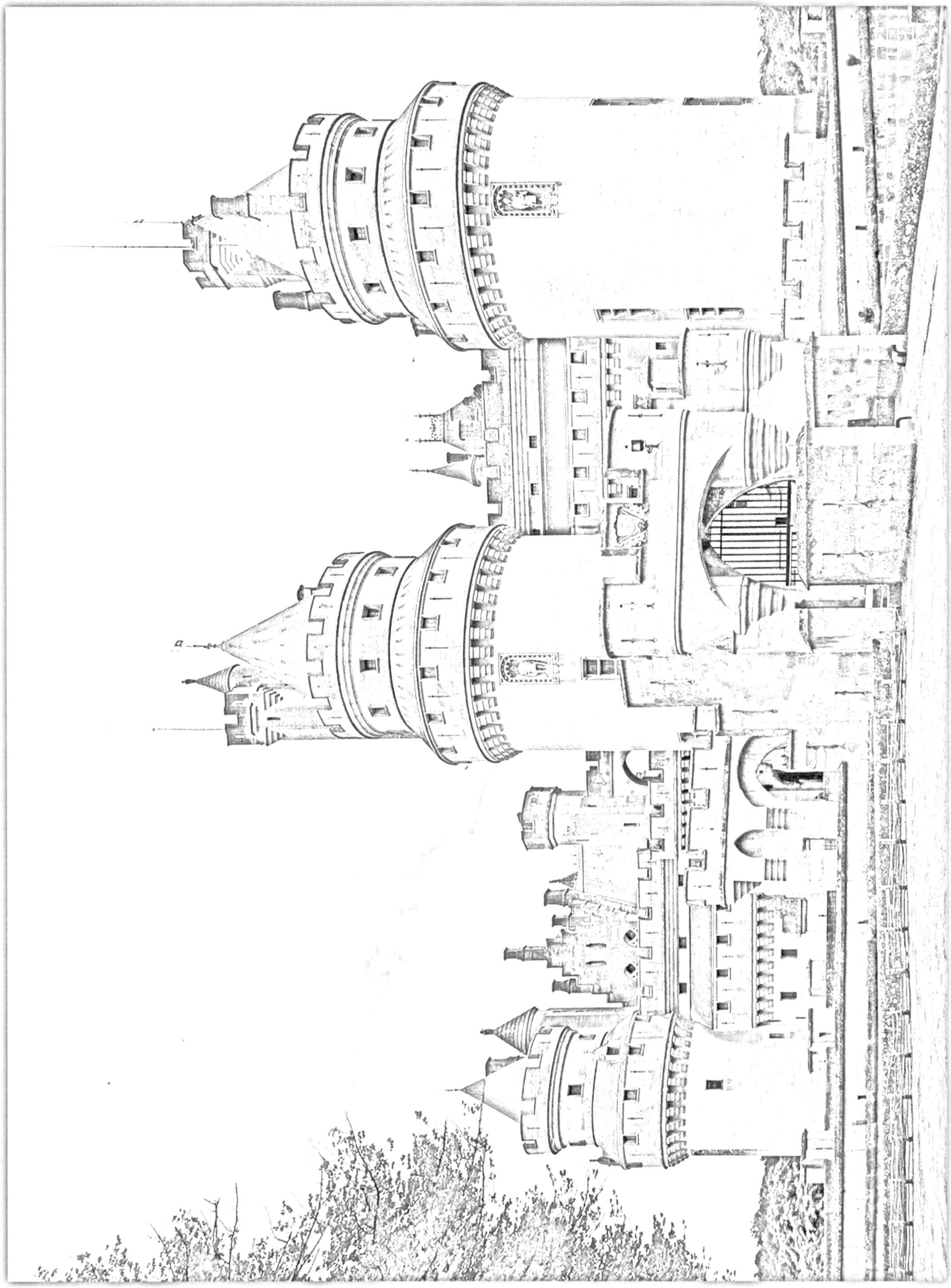

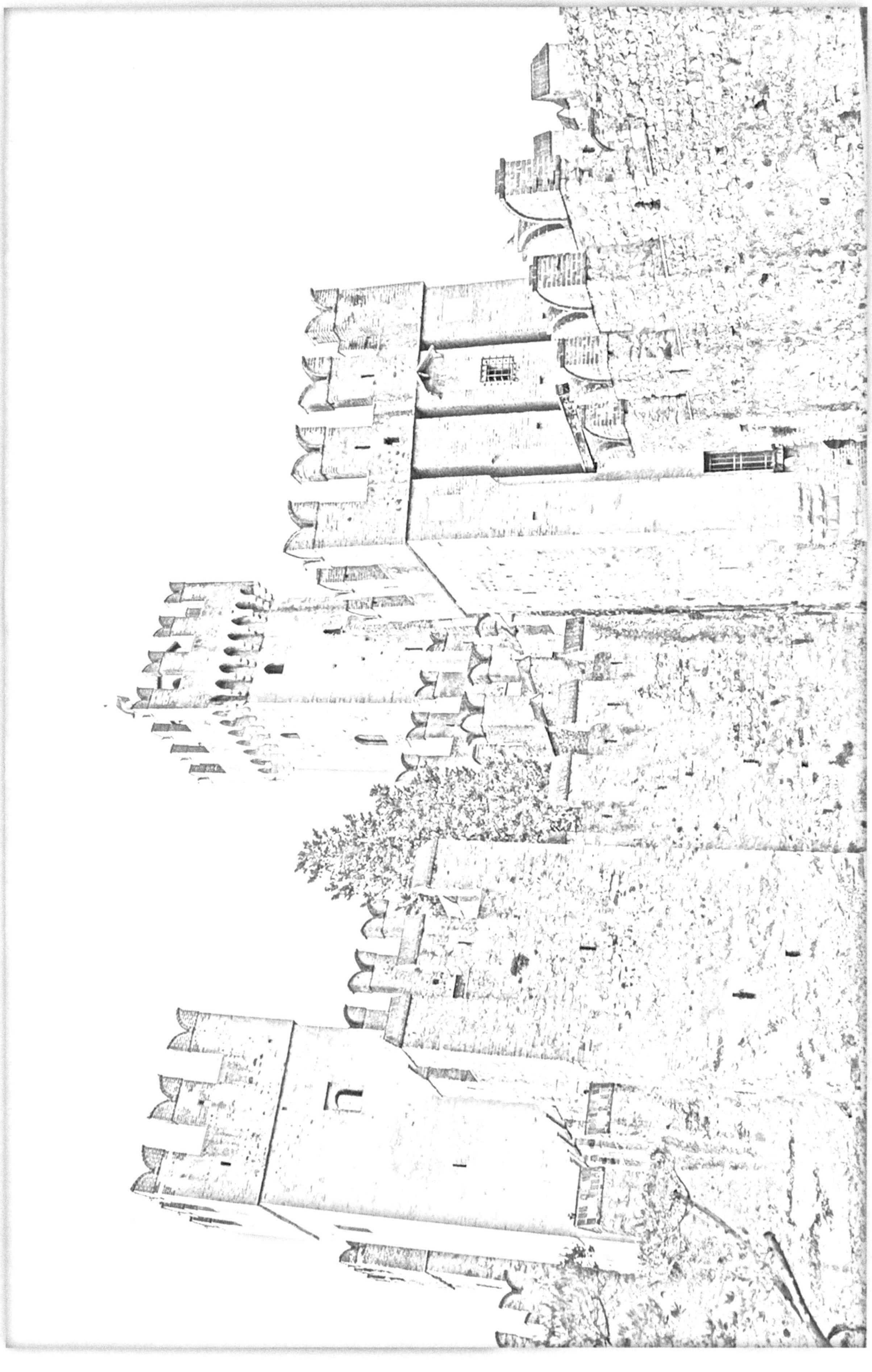

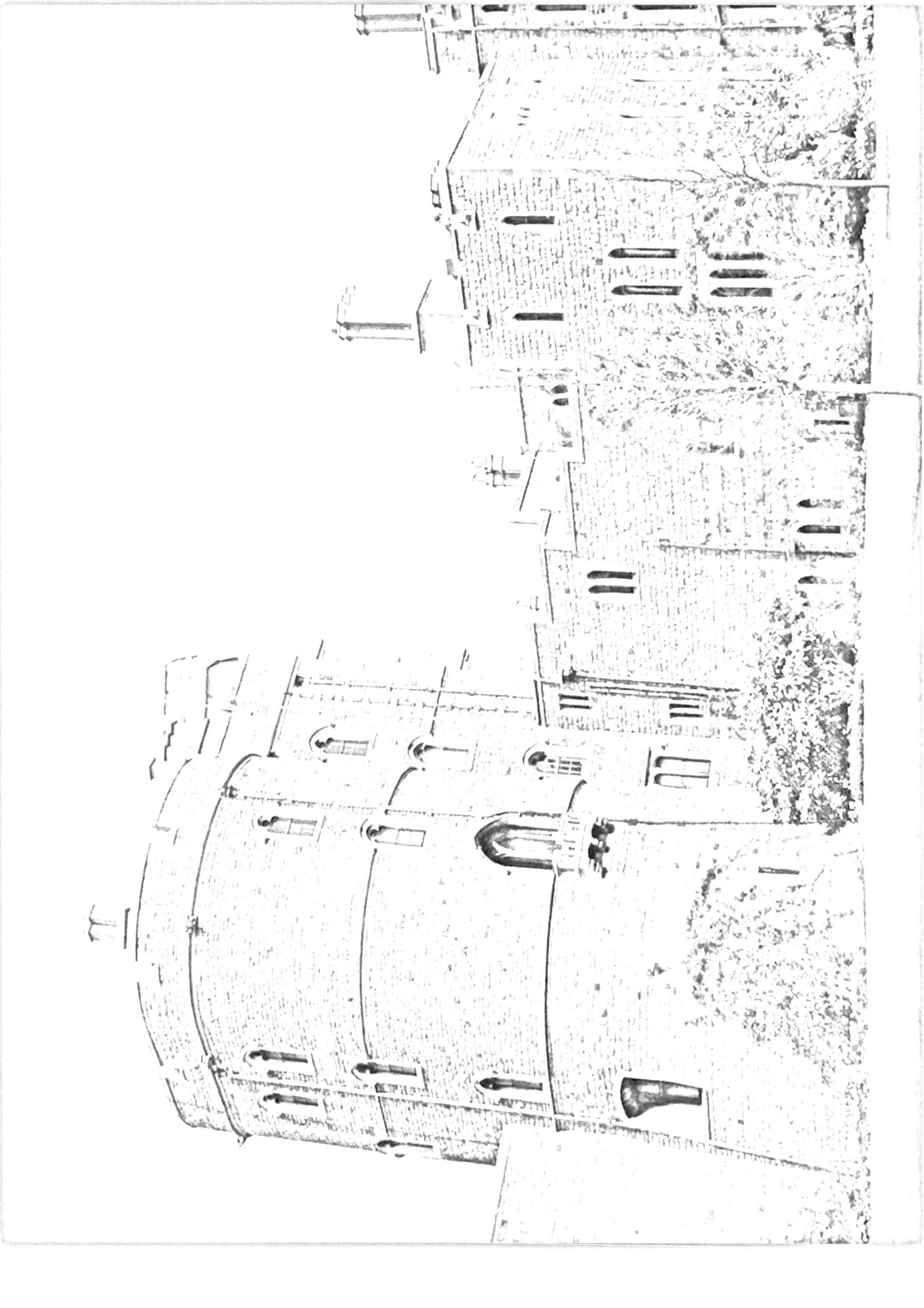

www.ingramcontent.com/pod-product-compliance
Lightning Source LLC
Chambersburg PA
CBHW041523280526
45792CB00004B/1359
* 9 7 8 1 5 2 3 8 3 9 1 1 7 *